The Usborne
Little Book
of
Flowers

First published in 2005 by Usborne Publishing Ltd.,
Usborne House, 83-85 Saffron Hill, London EC1N 8RT, England.
www.usborne.com

Main illustrations and borders copyright © 2005 by Petula Stone

UE. First published in America 2005
Printed in the UAE

The Usborne
Little Book
of
Flowers

Laura Howell

Designed by Joanne Kirkby and Michael Hill
Illustrated by Petula Stone
Digital illustration by Keith Furnival

Consultants: Dr Margaret Rostron
and Katherine Kear

Edited by Kirsteen Rogers

Internet links

There are lots of fun websites where you can find out more about flowers. We have created links to some of the best sites on the Usborne Quicklinks Website. To visit the sites, go to www.usborne-quicklinks.com and type the keywords "little book of flowers". Here are some of the things you can do on the Internet:

- ✿ Create and explore virtual gardens
- ✿ Try out lots of flower crafts and activities
- ✿ Play garden games and watch flower movies
- ✿ Watch animations of scattering seeds

Flower pictures to download

Pictures marked with a ✳ in this book can be downloaded from the Usborne Quicklinks Website, and there are templates and decorated paper too. These pictures are for personal use only and must not be used for commercial purposes.

Internet safety

The websites recommended in Usborne Quicklinks are regularly reviewed. However, the content of a website may change at any time and Usborne Publishing is not responsible for the content of websites other than its own. We recommend that children are supervised while on the Internet.

Contents

A history of flowers

Flowers have played an important role in people's lives for thousands of years. They have formed part of festivals and rituals, inspired artists, poets and storytellers and even been used as charms for love and luck.

Flowers for all occasions

For many people, the most important feature of a flower is its beauty. This is why flowers are so popular as decorations or ornaments, and are given as gifts to cheer people up. But flowers have other more practical uses, too, as ingredients in perfumes, foods and medicines. You can find out more about these on pages 58–61.

Roses have been specially grown for their looks for over 5,000 years.

Flower symbols

Flowers have been used to symbolize feelings and ideas for many centuries. In the past, when most people couldn't read or write, flower symbolism was a language that everyone understood.

Lilies were used in religious paintings to stand for purity.

Flower emblems

Many countries, states and regions have their own floral emblems. Some are common flowers in that area, but others are connected with a historical person or event.

These are cornflowers. Emperor Wilhelm of Germany liked them so much, he made them the national flower.

Floral design

The pleasing shapes of flowers have always inspired artists and craftworkers. In 19th-century Britain, artist William Morris became well-known for basing his designs on flowers and plants.

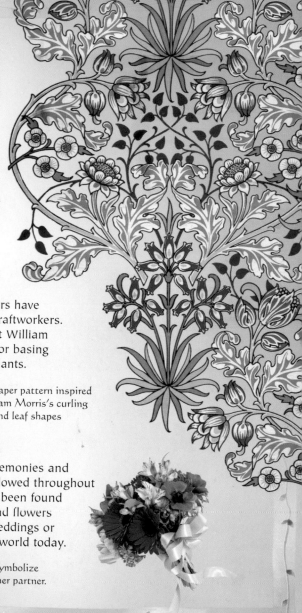

A wallpaper pattern inspired by William Morris's curling flower and leaf shapes

Flowers and rituals

Using flowers in religious ceremonies and other rituals is a tradition followed throughout history. Flower remains have been found in 60,000-year-old graves, and flowers are still given or carried at weddings or funerals in most parts of the world today.

The flowers in a wedding bouquet symbolize the bride's love and faithfulness to her partner.

Looking at flowers

Plants grow flowers as part of the process of making more plants like themselves. Flowers come in hundreds of shapes and sizes, and are found in most of the world's landscapes.

What do flowers do?

Flowers make tiny grains called pollen, which is carried to other flowers by insects and animals, or by the wind. The flower that receives it can then develop seeds, which will grow into new plants. Some flowers reward their visitors with a sweet liquid called nectar.

This anemone's bright petals attract insects.

Flower parts

Pollen is made by a flower's male parts, called stamens. Its female part, called the pistil, contains the structures that will later become seeds. Some flowers have only male or only female parts, but most have both.

You can see the pistil and stamens in the middle of the anemone.

Male and female parts vary in appearance from plant to plant. This is what an anemone's pistil and stamens look like close-up.

Bottlebrush flowers have hundreds of stamens.

A horned poppy has a long, slim pistil and small stamens.

Stamens

Pistil

Tree flowers

Most people think of flowers as growing on small plants, but trees produce them too. In spring, many grow delicate blossoms, which later turn into fruits, nuts or berries. These hold seeds inside, protected by juicy layers or a hard shell.

These white blossoms will one day produce apples.

Survival skills

Most experts think that flowering plants first grew over 130 million years ago. Today, there are around 270,000 types around the world. They have survived so well, and spread so far, because of their ability to thrive in the unlikeliest of places.

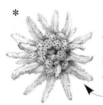

European edelweiss lives on cold, dry mountains. It has a thick layer of hairs to trap heat and water.

Water hyacinths have swollen, air-filled leaves, allowing them to float on water.

This rainforest orchid gets the light it needs by attaching itself to a branch near the top of a tree.

Flower features

If you want to identify a plant that you've found, look at where it grows, the number of flowers it has, and the shape and arrangement of its petals and leaves. You can then look it up in a field guide, or on the Internet.

Height and width

Flowers can grow up into the air, or creep sideways and cover the ground. A plant that spreads out like this is called a mat-forming plant.

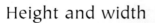

Many garden flowers, like these lupins, grow upright.

Flowers and stems

Plants might have one flower on a single stem, or many small flowers growing in a bunch.

Primroses have one flower per stem.

Rock cress has flowers in bunches.

Flowers within flowers

Sometimes, what you might think is a single flower is actually made up of lots of smaller flowers, called florets.

Asters are made up of many florets.

*

The florets in the middle are tiny yellow flowers.

This creeping jenny is a mat-forming plant.

Each floret around the outside has one long petal.

Location

Most flowers need certain conditions in order to grow well. For instance, they might prefer a shady rather than a sunny place, or damp soil rather than dry.

Bluebells usually grow in ancient woodlands, because they like the rich soil that's found there.

A bluebell's curled petals are joined together.

Looking at petals

The number, size and shapes of petals vary from flower to flower. Many have a scent or pattern to attract bugs or animals.

This orchid's patterned petals lure insects to it.

This petal is called a hood.

Insects land on this petal, the lip.

*

All the petals together are called the corolla. They can be separate, or joined in a bell or trumpet shape.

This rock rose has five separate petals.

Beardtongue flowers have joined petals.

Leaves

If you find a plant whose flowers have not yet opened, you might still be able to identify it by the look of its leaves. See if they have one overall shape, or are made up of several parts. Sometimes, there are many tiny leaves on one stalk.

Each of these bugle leaves is one large shape.

A wood anemone's leaf divides into three parts, joined at the base.

Partridge-pea flowers have little leaves, called leaflets, on a single stalk.

Shapes and edges

Leaves come in many different shapes, and their outlines can be smooth, wavy, sharp or jagged.

Pheasant's eye flowers have feathery leaves.

Lesser celandine has smooth, heart-shaped leaves.

Toothed leaves, like a wild strawberry's, are jagged.

A flowering currant's leaves are lobed, which means they are partially divided.

Winter squill leaves are entire (not toothed or lobed).

Sea holly's leaves are spiky.

Leaf arrangements

Look out for the different ways in which leaves can be arranged on the stem of a plant.

The leaves of a pussy paw form a rosette at the base of its stem.

Rose-pink leaves grow in opposite pairs.

The leaves of an ice plant grow up the stem in a pattern like a spiral staircase.

Wood lily leaves grow in rings called whorls.

Scarlet paintbrush leaves grow alternately on each side of the stem.

Leaf rubbing

Leaves from garden flowers can be used to make decorative leaf rubbings.

You will need:

✿ plain paper ✿ pencils or crayons ✿ clean, dry leaves

1. Place one or more leaves on a sheet of paper.

2. Carefully place more paper on top. Rub gently on it with a crayon.

You could arrange several leaves in a pattern before rubbing them.

How flowers grow

Most flowering plants start life as seeds. These sprout into shoots, and eventually grow flowers, which in turn make more seeds so the whole cycle can start again. This page shows how a poppy grows.

Bud

Most types of flowers develop in the same way as poppies.

1. In the spring, a poppy plant grows from a seed. First, it grows leaves. Then, buds start to form, with flowers furled up inside them.

2. Each flower is protected by tough sepals. These begin to part as the flower grows.

Each poppy bud has two spiky sepals.

Common poppy

3. In the summer, the flower's petals open out. You can see its male and female parts – the stamens and pistil – in the middle.

The pistil has two parts: a sticky stigma on top, and an ovary beneath.

Stamens

Pistil

Stigma

Ovary

Anther

Pollen grains

Filament

Stamens have pod-like anthers on the end of long, spindly filaments. The anthers open to release grains of pollen.

4. Bees and other pollen-carriers are attracted to poppies by their bright red petals. Pollen from the anthers sticks to the bee's hairy body as it crawls over the flower.

5. If the bee visits another poppy, the pollen may rub off its body onto the other flower's stigma. The next page shows what happens after this stage, which is called pollination, has taken place.

6. When grains of poppy pollen land on another poppy's stigma, very thin tubes begin to grow out of them, down to the ovary.

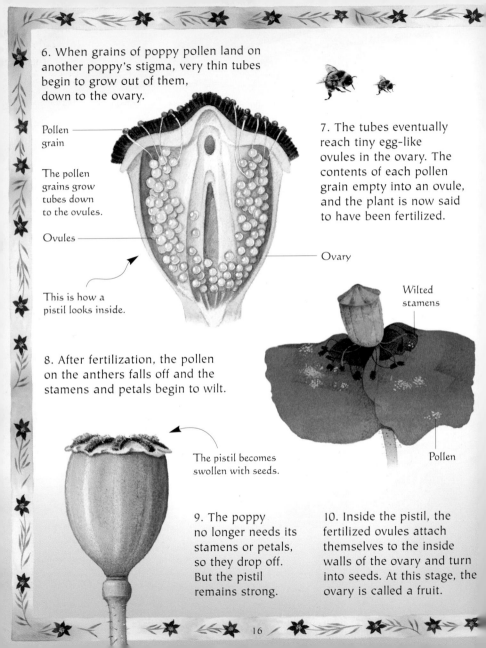

Pollen grain

The pollen grains grow tubes down to the ovules.

Ovules

This is how a pistil looks inside.

Ovary

7. The tubes eventually reach tiny egg-like ovules in the ovary. The contents of each pollen grain empty into an ovule, and the plant is now said to have been fertilized.

Wilted stamens

8. After fertilization, the pollen on the anthers falls off and the stamens and petals begin to wilt.

The pistil becomes swollen with seeds.

Pollen

9. The poppy no longer needs its stamens or petals, so they drop off. But the pistil remains strong.

10. Inside the pistil, the fertilized ovules attach themselves to the inside walls of the ovary and turn into seeds. At this stage, the ovary is called a fruit.

11. As the poppy fruit ripens, its outer case dries up. Holes appear at the top to let the seeds out.

Hole

Seeds

12. The seeds break away from the walls inside the fruit. When the poppy is blown about by the wind, the seeds are scattered like pepper from a pepper shaker.

13. Any seeds that fall out of the fruit onto the soil can grow into new plants next spring. These in turn will make seeds of their own.

Pollen from a poppy can't make seeds in buttercups, or any flower other than another poppy.

Spreading pollen

Most flowers can't pollinate themselves, because their stigmas and stamens ripen at different times. Instead, their pollen is carried off by animals, or by the wind.

Animal attraction

The strong, sweet smell of this stargazer lily lets passing insects know that it's worth paying a visit.

Patterns on the flower's petals, called nectar guides, show insects where to find the nectar.

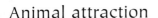

These spots and stripes are nectar guides.

Some types of flowers have nectar guides that only bees can see.

This evening primrose flower looks plain to you...

*

...but a bee's ultraviolet vision sees the nectar guides clearly.

A bird of paradise flower attracts birds. Its pollen sticks to their feet as they land.

*

Blowing in the wind

Flowers that rely on the wind to carry their pollen usually have uncovered stamens and pistils. Most of them hang loosely down, so it's easier for the wind to blow them about.

Each of these catkins is made up of dozens of tiny flowers. They give out lots of pollen, to increase the chances of it being blown to the right place.

Self-pollination

A few kinds of flowers use insects, but can also pollinate themselves.

Pollen sacs

Stamens

Male Eucera bee

The stigma is hidden inside.

1. Bee orchids look and smell like female Eucera bees. Male bees are attracted to them.

2. When a male bee visits an orchid, pollen sacs stick to his head. He will carry this pollen to another orchid.

3. If no bees come, the orchid pollinates itself. Its stamens bend over, so the pollen sacs can touch the stigma.

Pollen protection

Flowers can't reproduce without their pollen, so they use clever tricks to keep it safe and dry, and make sure that only the right kind of animals take it away.

Garden guardians

Some flowers only open when the weather is warm and sunny. They close up again if it looks like rain.

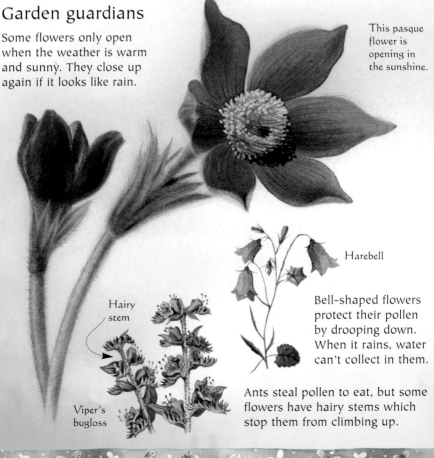

This pasque flower is opening in the sunshine.

Harebell

Hairy stem

Viper's bugloss

Bell-shaped flowers protect their pollen by drooping down. When it rains, water can't collect in them.

Ants steal pollen to eat, but some flowers have hairy stems which stop them from climbing up.

Invitation only

Some flowers only allow certain kinds of visitors, or can only be pollinated at a particular time.

Penstemon flowers

Stamens

Pollen rubs off on the hummingbird's head as it feeds.

Trumpet-shaped flowers are pollinated by hummingbirds and other creatures with long tongues. Pollen rubs off on their bodies as they reach in to drink the nectar.

Long-nosed bat

Hummingbird hawk moth

Honeysuckle

Most types of agave plant are pollinated only by bats with long, bristly tongues for lapping up nectar.

Agave flower

Broom flower

Honeysuckle flowers open in the evening, when the moths that pollinate them are awake. Their strong scent makes them easy to find in the dark.

Broom flowers stay tightly shut when small insects land on them. But if a heavy bumblebee stops by, its weight is enough to make the flower open up.

Scattering seeds

Seeds need light to grow, so they must be carried away from the shadow of their parent plant to survive. You might see seeds flying through the air, hitch-hiking on animals and people, or floating down a stream.

Flying away

Some seeds have natural parachute, balloon or wing-like shapes. These float in the wind.

Dandelion seeds are inside tiny fruits attached to fluffy parachutes.

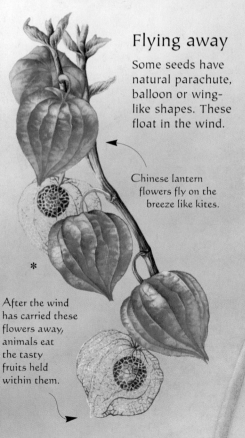

Chinese lantern flowers fly on the breeze like kites.

*

After the wind has carried these flowers away, animals eat the tasty fruits held within them.

Burdock seeds

Sticking on

Some seeds have burrs or hooks. They stick to animals, which carry them far away.

Tasty seeds

Birds and other animals eat fruits with seeds inside. Later, the seeds fall to the ground in their droppings.

This raccoon will spread the tree's seeds by eating its fruit.

Popping out

Some types of fruits burst open to shoot seeds out.

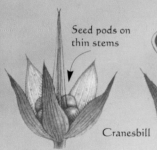

Seed pods on thin stems

Cranesbill

Seed

The stems curl up and shoot the seeds out of their pods.

On the water

A few types of seeds are carried away by oceans and rivers, inside floating pods.

Alder tree

Seeds fall in the water and float away.

People and seeds

People help to spread seeds too, often without even knowing. Seeds stick in the soles of shoes, or on car wheels.

In the garden

People have kept gardens for thousands of years. In the past, they were used to grow plants for food or medicine. Today, though, gardens are more likely to be full of flowers, which are grown for their appearance and scent.

Ornamental flowers

Many people like to grow ornamental flowers. These have been carefully bred to improve their shape and size, and they usually bloom for longer than their wild relatives.

Wild roses have fewer petals than ornamental ones.

This tea rose was cultivated for its many delicate layers of pink petals.

Wild flowers

If something grows without being planted, it's probably a wild flower. Some types are harmless, but others spread very fast, stealing water and light from other plants. They are known as weeds.

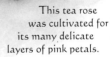

Bindweed looks pretty, but its creeping stems choke other plants.

Types of flowers

When you're choosing what to plant in your garden, it helps to know what will bloom when. The three main kinds of flowering plants are annuals, biennials and perennials.

Plants that live and die in a single year are called annuals. Some grow, spread pollen and make seeds in as little as a week.

The seeds of annual plants, such as this petunia, stay buried in the ground over winter, and grow in the spring.

*

Biennials develop over two years. They grow in the first year, then make flowers and seeds in the second.

This wallflower is in its second year. The whole plant dies after it has made its seeds.

Plants that live for many years are called perennials.

Bellflowers are perennials. They regrow from roots each year.

Trees and shrubs, such as this buddleia, are perennials whose trunks and stems don't die each year.

Some perennials live underground as roots during winter, and grow new stems in the spring. Others keep their stems and trunks as well as their roots.

Garden wildlife

Flowers attract all kinds of insects and animals to your garden. Some are harmful, but most help the plants in some way.

Pollen sticks to a honeybee's fuzzy body as it crawls over a flower.

Garden friends

Bees are good at spreading pollen, because they gather nectar from a single type of flower per trip. This increases the chances of fertilization happening. Butterflies are also helpful pollen spreaders, because they pollinate some types of flowers that bees don't often visit.

Birds feed on fruits and spread their seeds, which makes them useful garden visitors. Some also eat garden pests, such as snails and slugs.

A butterfly can unfurl its tube-like mouthparts to reach deeper into flowers than bees can.

Garden enemies

Some bugs damage plants by eating their buds and leaves, or laying their eggs on them.

Aphids give birth to dozens of babies, which suck the juices out of flower buds.

Caterpillars harm plants by chewing their leaves, but adult moths help plants by spreading pollen.

Attracting wildlife

You can invite helpful animals to your garden by planting the kinds of flowers that they like best. A mixture of plants will attract many different species.

Birds eat the juicy berries that grow on trees and shrubs.

Fieldfare eating rowan tree berries

To attract moths, plant flowers that bloom or release their scent at night, such as honeysuckle or evening primrose.

Peacock butterfly

Sweet-smelling snapdragons, ice plants and buddleias appeal to bees and butterflies.

This honeysuckle's scent has attracted an elephant hawk moth.

A heart and dart moth is visiting this evening primrose.

Red admiral

Many butterflies are attracted by the scent of ice plants.

Growing sunflowers

Sunflowers attract bees and butterflies to your garden, and provide birds with tasty seeds to eat. If you plant seeds in early spring, you should have flowers by September.

You will need:

✿ small and large pots with holes in the bottom
✿ packet of sunflower seeds ✿ watering can
✿ potting compost ✿ small stones
✿ garden cane ✿ string or twine

Watering can

1. Put a handful of stones in the bottom of a small pot, and fill it with potting compost.

2. Press three or four sunflower seeds firmly into the compost.

3. Water the pot and put it outside in a light spot. Water it regularly so the compost doesn't dry out.

Small seedling

Large seedlings

4. A seedling should grow from each of the seeds. Take out all but the biggest two, so they have room to grow.

5. When the seedlings have grown about as tall as your hand, replant them into bigger pots.

6. Water your plants and leave them in a sunny place, out of the wind.

Twine

Cane

7. When the plants are about knee-high, push a cane into the compost in each pot. Tie the stems loosely on.

Some sunflowers can grow taller than a person. Check the seed packet to see what height yours might reach.

8. As the sunflowers grow taller, carefully tie their stems higher up the canes.

9. When the petals have fallen off, birds will eat the seeds in the middle.

Winter pansies

Pansies grow in cold weather, so you can use them to add a splash of brightness to a winter garden. They come in many shades, including purple, burgundy and gold.

When to plant

If you'd like to see winter flowers, sow your seeds in late summer. Some types of pansies should be sown in spring, so check the seed packet.

You will need:

✿ cardboard egg carton
✿ potting compost ✿ pansy seeds
✿ teaspoon ✿ strainer
✿ newspaper ✿ some pots

Egg carton

1. Dip the bottom half of the carton in a bowl of water and let it drip.

2. Spoon compost into each section, but not all the way to the top.

Strainer

3. Put two pansy seeds in each section. Sprinkle more compost on top.

Water the seeds regularly.

4. Cover the seeds with a newspaper. Keep them indoors in a cool spot.

Shoots

5. When shoots grow, remove the paper to give them lots of light.

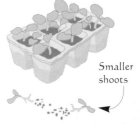

Smaller shoots

6. When each shoot has two leaves, pull out the smaller of the two shoots

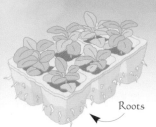

Roots

7. As your pansies grow, roots will sprout through the sides of the carton.

Handle the carton carefully as you pull.

8. Soak the carton in shallow water and gently pull the sections apart.

9. Put each section into a pot half-filled with compost. Fill in with more compost.

When flowers have started to grow, move your pots outside.

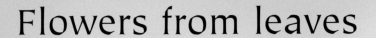

Flowers from leaves

In the right conditions, some plants can grow from a single leaf. Snipping a piece off a healthy plant and using it to create a new one is called taking a cutting, and it's a fun way to share plants with your friends.

You will need:

❀ African violet plant ❀ paper square ❀ scissors
❀ small bottle ❀ rubber band ❀ sharp pencil
❀ pot with holes in the bottom ❀ potting compost

1. Fill a small bottle with water. Don't fill it quite to the top.

2. Fasten the paper square over the top with a rubber band.

Choose a healthy-looking leaf from near the outside of the plant.

Scissors

Cut leaf

3. Use scissors to cut off a leaf, complete with its stalk, from an African violet plant.

Pencil

5. Hold the bottle and use the pencil to poke a hole in the middle of the paper.

6. Push the stalk through the hole until its end is in the water.

Keep your plant in a place with lots of light.

Roots

7. When tiny roots grow and new leaves appear, your leaf is ready to plant in a pot.

8. Fill the pot with compost, make a hole and put the plant in. Press the compost firmly all around.

9. Place the pot on a saucer. Water the plant by pouring water into the saucer.

Spring bulbs

Some plants grow from bulbs instead of seeds. A bulb has layers of tightly packed leaves inside, which store food for the plant. For spring flowers, plant bulbs in the autumn.

You will need:

- ✿ bulbs, such as crocus or daffodil
- ✿ frost-proof terracotta pot, three-quarters full of potting compost
- ✿ small stick ✿ trowel

Miniature daffodil

Crocus

Shoots appear first, then flowers will begin to grow after about 10–12 weeks.

1. Using the stick, make a hole in the compost for each bulb

2. Rest the fat end of the bulbs in the holes.

3. Cover the bulbs with compost and put the pot outside.

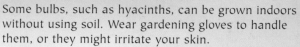

Some bulbs, such as hyacinths, can be grown indoors without using soil. Wear gardening gloves to handle them, or they might irritate your skin.

When your bulb flowers, you can plant it in a pot. Keep it indoors.

You will need:

✿ gardening gloves
✿ a hyacinth bulb
✿ three toothpicks
✿ a glass jar

Toothpick

1. Push toothpicks into the bulb. Fill the jar almost to the top with water.

2. Rest the toothpicks on the rim, so the bulb's fat end is near the water.

Roots

3. Leave the jar in a cool, dark place out of the frost, such as a shed.

4. After roots have grown, leaves will sprout. Move the jar to a light, cool spot.

A miniature garden

If you'd like to see flowers without waiting for them to grow, you could buy ready-grown plants and make a mini garden.

You will need:

❀ plastic tray or bowl ❀ bag of small pebbles ❀ stones
❀ potting compost ❀ trowel ❀ gravel ❀ small plants and flowers
such as pansies, primulas, ivy, trailing lobelia and fittonia

1. Using the trowel, cover the bottom of the tray with about 2cm (1in) of pebbles.

2. Cover the layer of pebbles with potting compost. Fill the tray almost to the top.

3. Decide how you're going to lay out your plants. Leave a gap down the middle for a path.

4. Make holes in the compost for each plant. Take them from their pots and place them in.

5. Firmly press a little compost around each plant. Water them to help them settle.

6. Use the gravel to make a winding path through your garden. Add larger stones for decoration.

Garden care

Keep your garden indoors out of direct sunlight. Water it every other day, adding a little plant food to the water occasionally to help keep your plants healthy. If any plants grow too big for the tray, replant them into a larger pot.

A garden pond

If you like, you could add a pond to your garden by making a hole in the compost and putting in a plastic carton of water.

Put a little gravel in the carton, and fill it with water to make a pond.

Kalanchoe

Parlour palms

Primula flowers come in many shades.

Fittonia

Primulas

Trailing plants, such as ivy, hang over the sides.

This garden is decorated with stones, but you could also use toys, shells, or shiny glass pebbles.

Flower art

Flower shapes can be used to make pictures, or decorate cards, folders and diaries. Here are two easy types to create.

To make two-tone flowers, you will need:

❀ thick white paper ❀ water-based paints
❀ paintbrush with soft bristles
❀ jar of water

Use slightly watery paint.

Add the second shade quickly, while the petals are still wet.

The leaves should be near the petals, but not touching them.

1. Paint five blobs for petals, leaving a thin gap between them.

2. Add a contrasting shade of paint on each petal near the middle.

3. When the petals are dry, add leaves, and a blob in the middle.

Experiment with different paint shades.

Leave a thin white border around the flowers as you cut.

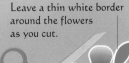

4. When all the paint has dried, cut the flowers and leaves out.

To make paper pansies, you will need:

❀ pink, purple, yellow, green and black tissue paper ❀ white paper or
thin cardboard ❀ glue ❀ scissors ❀ clean jar ❀ paintbrush

Make the purple and pink pieces the size of a large coin.

Leave a little white area around the yellow paper.

1. Tear round shapes out of the pink, purple, black and yellow tissue paper.

2. Put a little glue in the jar. Add a few drops of water and stir.

3. Glue a small yellow piece to the paper. Glue two pink pieces above it.

Pansy leaves are heart shaped, like this.

4. Glue one purple piece on either side of the yellow paper, then a bigger one beneath.

5. Glue black pieces onto the petals. Cut out leaf shapes and stick them around the flowers.

Other pansy petal combinations that work well are yellow and blue, and red and orange.

Pop-up flowers

Give your friends a surprise with this
pop-up flower display in a greeting card.

You will need:

❀ pieces of bright, stiff paper 18x28cm (7x11in), 8x10cm (3x4in) and
6x6cm (2.5x2.5in) ❀ extra sheet of paper ❀ painted flowers or flowers
cut from magazines and giftwrap ❀ glue ❀ scissors ❀ ruler

The largest piece (A)
will be your card.

Make each of these flaps
1cm (0.5in) wide.

Glue

Match up the creases.

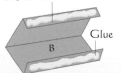

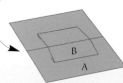

1. Fold the largest (A)
and medium-sized (B)
pieces of paper in the
middle. Open them out.

2. Make folds on the
ends of the medium
paper (B). Add glue to
the flaps' outer sides.

3. Turn piece B over
with the flaps tucked
under and press it flat
on the card's middle.

Match the crease on piece
C with the top of piece B.

Find out how to paint flowers
like these on page 38.

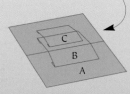

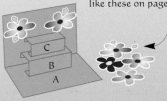

4. Repeat step 2 with
the smallest paper (C).
Glue it on top of piece
B and leave it to dry.

5. Glue a selection of
cut-out flowers and
leaves onto the card
above piece C.

Don't let any flowers overlap this edge.

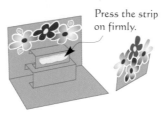

Press the strip on firmly.

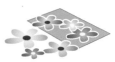

6. Cut out a piece of paper 5x9cm (2x3.5in). Glue flowers all over, except one long edge.

7. Glue the front of piece C. Press the paper strip onto it, with the straight edge at the bottom.

8. Cut out a piece of paper 5x12cm (2x5in). Glue flowers onto it, as shown in step 6.

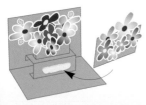

9. Glue the front of piece B. Press the flowery strip firmly onto it, and leave all the glue to dry.

Decorate a fancy envelope to put your card inside.

You could glue flowers on the front of the card too.

Paper roses

A bouquet of handmade roses is a long-lasting and less expensive alternative to real ones. Red traditionally stands for love, but you could also use pink, yellow or white paper.

You will need:

❀ red crêpe paper ❀ green crêpe paper ❀ florist's wire
❀ thin wire (e.g. from a hardware store) ❀ thread
❀ glue ❀ pencil ❀ scissors ❀ ruler

Long, folded edge

Short side

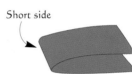

1. Cut out a 12x35cm (5x14in) strip of red tissue paper. Fold the long sides together.

2. Open it out and glue the lower half. Press the halves together, then let them dry.

3. With the long, folded edge nearest to you, fold the paper in half from left to right three times.

Don't cut the bottom edge.

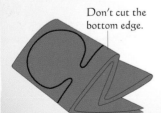

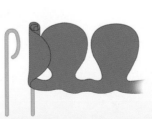

Thread

4. Draw a petal shape as shown here and cut around it. Carefully unfold it.

5. Bend one end of the florist's wire into a small loop. Roll the first two petals tightly around it.

6. Wrap the other petals less tightly, pinching them at the base. Tie with thread.

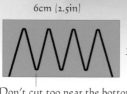

6cm (2.5in)

3cm (1in)

Don't cut too near the bottom.

7. To make sepals, which go beneath the petals, draw this pattern on the green paper and cut it out. Use the lower part.

Glue

8. Put glue on the straight edge and wind it tightly around the base of the petals.

9. To make a leaf, cut out two leaf shapes like these. Glue them together with thin wire in the middle.

You'll need to repeat steps one to twelve for every rose that you make.

10. Repeat step 9 to make another leaf. Put the two side by side and twist the wires together.

Long paper strip for stem

11. For the stem, cut a strip of paper 1.5cm (0.5in) wide. Glue one end to the sepals.

Leaf wires

12. Twist the leaf wires onto the stem 4cm (1.5in) down. Wind the paper down over them.

Pressing flowers

Most flowers have short lives, but pressing them is a way to preserve them for longer. You can press leaves, too. Stick your flowers and leaves on a diary or notebook, or use them to decorate cards.

You will need:

✿ small, open-faced flowers ✿ leaves
✿ heavy books ✿ blotting paper ✿ tweezers

Pressed
verbenas

Selecting flowers

Choose clean, healthy blooms with no ugly marks. Look carefully at the edges of the petals and leaves to make sure they haven't been nibbled by bugs or slugs.

Press the flowers soon after picking them. Never pick wild flowers – there won't be any left for other people to enjoy. If you prefer, you could buy some flowers to press.

Pressed viola
flowers and
a fern leaf

Pick flowers
on a sunny
day, when
they're dry.

1. Use fresh flowers that have fully opened. Pick the flowerhead, along with a small length of stem.

Use an old book, in case
the petals stain the pages.

2. Put paper on one page
of an open book. Lay the
flowers flat on the paper,
a little distance apart.

3. Lay another piece
of paper over the flowers.
Smooth it down gently,
then close the book.

4. Stack more books on
top. Leave the flowers in
the book for at least two
weeks to dry and flatten.

Look for flowers
that are naturally
flat, such as violas,
petunias and
primulas like these.
Bulky flowers don't
press as easily.

Protecting your flowers

Pressed flowers are very fragile and
tear easily, so use tweezers to pick them
up. Your flowers will fade or turn brown
naturally over time, but if you keep them
out of direct sunlight, they will
stay brighter for longer.

With a little care,
flowers will keep
their looks for a
long time after
being pressed.

Using pressed flowers

You can use pressed flowers to decorate all kinds of things, such as cards, bookmarks and gift tags. Press them yourself (see page 44), or buy pre-pressed flowers from craft stores.

You will need:

❀ thin cardboard ❀ pressed flowers and leaves ❀ tweezers ❀ glue
❀ hole punch ❀ scissors ❀ clear book-covering film

1. Cut out shaped pieces of cardboard to make your gift tags and bookmarks.

2. Use tweezers to lay the flowers and leaves on the cardboard. Try out different arrangements.

3. Dab a dot of glue on the back of each flower and leaf, then stick them down.

Gift tags

To turn your cardboard shape into a gift tag, use the hole punch to make a hole in the top. Thread a ribbon through the hole to tie the tag to a gift.

Cut your gift tags in various shapes, such as hearts, circles and blossoms.

Bookmarks

Stick small, delicate flowers and leaves to strips of cardboard to make bookmarks. You can make the flowers last longer if you cover the front of the cardboard in clear book-covering film.

Cut the film sticky-side up.

Peel the backing from the film and lay it on the front of the bookmark. Smooth it out, turn it over, and cut around the edge.

Pressed rosebuds

Pretty pictures

Try arranging lots of one type of flower in a pattern, such as a circle or a ladder-like shape. You could also experiment with flowers and leaves to make a bouquet design.

Tie some ribbon in a bow to decorate your bouquet.

You can print out templates for making bookmarks, gift tags and picture frames on the Usborne Quicklinks Website at www.usborne-quicklinks.com.

Put your flower picture in a frame or cardboard mount.

Everlasting flowers

Flowers with small, stiff leaves or large seed pods can be dried to preserve their looks, sometimes for many years. This works because a flower can't rot when it's lost all its moisture.

You will need:

❁ assorted flowers ❁ rubber bands
❁ string ❁ scissors

Pick long-stemmed flowers, a little before they're fully open.

Dried statice, amaranthus and strawflowers

1. Pick flowers on a clear day, once any dew has dried. Sort each type of flower into a separate bunch.

2. Strip the lower leaves off the stems. Fasten each bunch of flowe together tightly with a rubber banc

Ears of corn

You could also try drying grasses, berries or seed pods. Some work better than others, so experiment with different things.

Berry sprig

Poppy seed heads

3. Fan the flower heads out a little so that they aren't touching each other. This stops them from rotting.

Keep the flowers hanging until the stems are completely stiff.

Dried flowers are delicate, so handle them carefully when you arrange them.

4. Hang the bunches from the string in a warm, airy place away from direct sunlight, such as a garage.

5. Display your dried flowers in a basket, jug or vase, so you can see the flowers but not the stems.

Lucky flowers

Some flowers are associated with a particular month of the year. It's said that the flower of the month you were born in will bring you good luck.

January: Snowdrop
Snowdrops are one of the earliest flowers to grow after the cold of winter. For this reason, they symbolize hope.

*

February: Violet
Garlands of violets used to be given to children for luck on their third birthday.

*

March: Daffodil
Daffodils are a traditional Easter bloom, and also the national flower of Wales.

*

April: Sweet pea
The sweet pea is commonly known as the queen of annuals.

May: Lily of the Valley
In France, it's believed that giving someone a lily on the first day of May will bring luck all year.

*

June: Rose
Roses are age-old symbols of love and beauty. They're also linked to royalty and religion.

*

July: Water lily or lotus
The lotus is a sacred flower in Hinduism and Buddhism, because it represents purity and perfection.

*

August: Gladiolus
The blade-like shape of its leaves inspired this flower's name, which means "sword" in Latin.

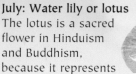

September: Morning glory
Morning glories take their name from the fact that they open in the morning. Each flower blooms for one day, then dies.

*

*

October: Cosmos
"Cosmos" means "orderly universe". This flower came to represent order because of its evenly spaced petals.

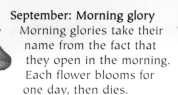

November: Chrysanthemum
Chrysanthemums are the national flower of Japan, where they represent both the Sun and life itself.

*

*

December: Holly
Ancient monks believed that holly could repel evil.

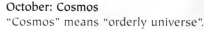

Flower language

In England, during Queen Victoria's reign, the "language of flowers" was a very popular idea. Giving a particular type of flower was a way of passing on a secret message to a friend or sweetheart.

Sharing feelings

In the 19th century, it was considered rude to talk openly about your feelings. Using flowers allowed people to express their emotions without speaking. Here are just a few of the hundreds of blooms that were given a meaning.

Cabbage flowers revealed that you would profit from something.

*

Rhododendrons were used to warn a lover of danger.

Star-of-Bethlehem flowers were a symbol of purity.

White stonecrop flowers represented calmness.

As you might think, forget-me-nots meant you wanted to be remembered.

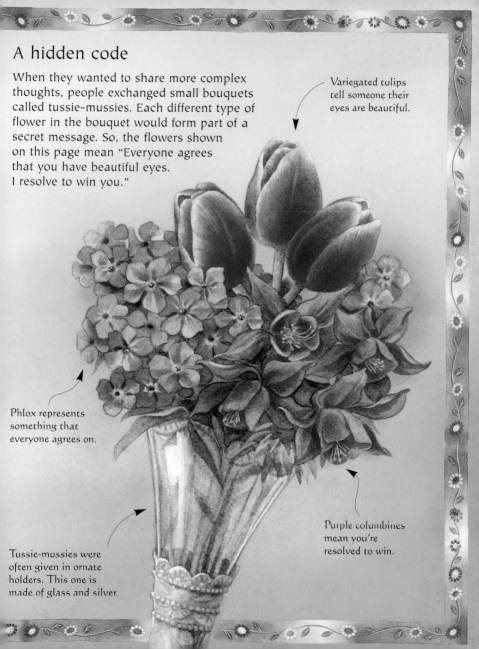

A hidden code

When they wanted to share more complex thoughts, people exchanged small bouquets called tussie-mussies. Each different type of flower in the bouquet would form part of a secret message. So, the flowers shown on this page mean "Everyone agrees that you have beautiful eyes. I resolve to win you."

Variegated tulips tell someone their eyes are beautiful.

Phlox represents something that everyone agrees on.

Tussie-mussies were often given in ornate holders. This one is made of glass and silver.

Purple columbines mean you're resolved to win.

Myths and legends

Many flowers take their names from ancient stories which explain how they came to exist, or why they look or grow the way they do.

Lady slippers

The lady slipper orchid's name comes from a Native American story. A young girl went to fetch medicine when the people of her village developed a terrible disease, but along the way, she lost her shoes in a blizzard. Although her feet were frozen and bleeding, she struggled on. Her courage saved the village, and, when the snow melted, shoe-shaped flowers bloomed in her footprints.

The lady slipper's spots are said to represent blood from the brave little girl's feet.

A Christmas tale

The legend of the Christmas rose begins at the birth of Jesus. When a shepherd girl cried at having no gift to give to the baby, an angel turned her tears into a bouquet of delicate white flowers.

Christmas roses bloom at Christmas time.

Greek myths

Iris flowers are named after the Greek goddess of the rainbow. Iris was said to have painted the sky with her rainbow, and crossed it to carry messages from heaven to Earth. Irises grew wherever her feet touched the ground.

The name "iris" literally means "eye of heaven".

Yarrow is also known as Achillea, after an ancient Greek hero named Achilles. It was said that he gave this plant to his soldiers to heal their wounds. Modern tests show that yarrow really does contain chemicals that stop blood from flowing.

Yarrow

Wild asters take their name from the Greek goddess Asterea. Legend has it that when she looked down on the Earth and saw no stars in the sky, her tears of sadness turned into star-shaped flowers.

According to an ancient Greek tale, Narcissus was the most handsome man in the world. He drowned while trying to kiss his reflection in a lake, but the gods turned him into a flower so his beauty would live on after his death.

"Aster" is the Latin word for "star".

Narcissus

Flower superstitions

People used to think that flowers could influence their future, bring good or bad luck and protect them from harm. Superstitions like these are found all over the world.

Arum lily

Rosemary planted by a door was thought to strengthen friendship.

Rosemary

Arum lilies, sometimes called death lilies, had a strange double meaning. In a bride's bouquet they were seen as lucky, but a bouquet of them in your home was said to invite death.

Farmers hung primroses in their cowsheds to stop fairies from stealing the milk.

Bad luck was believed to follow if all the petals fell from a freshly cut rose.

Rose

Snapdragon

Snapdragons were said to keep people safe from curses.

Primrose

Monkshood was believed to repel werewolves.

Monkshood is also known as wolfsbane.

It was once thought that if you cut a sunflower while making a wish, your wish would come true before the next sunset.

Sunflower

Another name for a viola is heart's-ease.

People used to think that violas could cure a broken heart, because their petals are heart-shaped.

Legend has it that adding cuckoo flowers to a May garland would bring the wearer bad luck, or even cause them to be carried away to Fairyland.

Cuckoo flowers

Daisy

Daisies are used in a traditional game to discover someone's feelings. The petals are picked one by one, while saying "loves me... loves me not". The last petal reveals if you are loved, or not.

Dreaming about daisies was thought to be lucky in spring or summer, but unlucky in autumn or winter.

Useful flowers

Flowers and plants that have a practical use are called herbs. In the past, most people grew their own herbs and used them to make food, drinks and medicines.

Herbal medicine

Before the 19th century, almost all diseases were treated using parts of plants. Many traditional remedies have been forgotten or are no longer thought to work, but others are still widely used.

*

St John's Wort has been used through the ages to ease depression.

*

People used to believe that drinking a potion of daisy juice for fifteen days cured insanity.

Although some ancient herbal remedies are based on superstition, there's no doubt that flowers can be used to make medicine. In fact, around a quarter of all modern drugs prescribed by doctors come from plants.

Foxgloves are the source of digitalis, a drug used to treat heart disease.

Kitchen herbs

Cooks have used the mouthwatering smell and taste of herbs for many centuries. Although the parts of the plant that are used today are mostly the leaves or roots, some types of flowers can safely be eaten too.

Nasturtium leaves and petals can be added to salads for a peppery taste.

Dried clove flower buds are used as a spice, often in cooked fruit dishes.

Spice it up

Spices are herbs with a particularly strong taste or smell. Many spices, such as nutmeg and vanilla, are made from a flower's seeds or seed pods.

Sweet dreams

Lavender is a herb whose scent brings peaceful sleep. Try making these decorative lavender bags and keeping them by your pillow.

You will need:

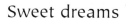

✿ dried lavender ✿ ribbon ✿ chalk
✿ scissors ✿ fabric ✿ a plate

You can buy dried lavender in health food stores, or dry some yourself.

Tie the ribbon into a bow.

Fabric circle

1. Draw around the plate with the chalk to make a circle. Cut it out.

2. Put a handful of lavender in the middle. Bunch up the fabric over the top.

3. Tightly tie a ribbon around the fabric to hold it together.

Sweet scents

The scent of a flower comes from oils in its petals.
This aroma has an important purpose in nature, and
people have many uses for fragrant flowers too.

Why do flowers smell?

In the natural world, flowers have
scent to attract pollen-carriers. Many
scented flowers have unpatterned
petals, because they
don't need bright
markings to lure
insects in.

Orange blossoms look
plain but smell luscious.

Not all flowers smell good – some
appeal to insects because they
smell of rotten meat or bad eggs.

A stapelia's
foul stink
attracts flies to
carry its pollen.

Scentless flowers

Some flowers don't need to attract
insects, so they have
no scent at all.

Ribwort plantain is
pollinated by the wind,
so it has no scent.

The history of perfume

The ancient Egyptians were the first
people known to make perfume from
flowers. They soaked their skin in
flower oils, and kept themselves
smelling attractive by melting cones of
animal fat and petals on their heads.

This ancient Egyptian painting shows women
wearing flower-scented cones in their hair.

Scenting the home

People use flowers to scent their homes as well as their bodies. In the past, they did this by scattering fresh herbs on the floor, which released their scent when crushed underfoot. Today, displays of dried or fresh flowers have the same purpose, but can be decorative too.

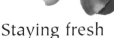

Staying fresh

Before cities had sewers, floral perfumes disguised the smell of dirty streets and homes, as well as smelly clothes. In the 18th century, rich people often walked around with balls of beeswax and petals called pomanders held under their noses, or carried on their sleeves.

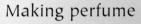

Many people scent their homes with potpourri, a mix of dried petals, fruits, leaves and herbs.

Making perfume

The simplest way to extract oil from petals involves boiling flowers and water. The mix gives out steam, which cools and becomes drops of water and flower oil. These can then be separated. A huge number of flowers is needed to obtain just a little oil, so the floral scents in most perfumes are made artificially.

Only the most expensive fragrances contain pure flower oils.

Flower facts

The biggest...
The world's largest flower is the rafflesia, which can reach up to 1m (3ft) across. It grows on tropical vines, stealing their food and water.

A rafflesia flower has thick, fleshy petals, but no leaves, stem or roots.

...and smallest
The smallest flowers in the world belong to a group of water plants called wolffia. One dozen of them would fit on a pinhead.

Extended families
The largest families of flowering plants are the sunflower family, with over 24,000 species, and the orchid family, with 20,000 species.

Orchids come in thousands of varieties.

*

Busy bees
Honey bees must gather nectar from two million flowers to make 500g (1lb) of honey.

Honey bees

Costly spice
The most expensive spice in the world is saffron. 250,000 crocus flower stamens are needed to make 500g (1lb) of it.

Crocus

Fascinating names
Peonies are one of the most highly valued flowers in the Far East. Their Chinese name is "sho yu", which means "most beautiful".

In Mexico, zinnias were originally called "mal de ojos", meaning "bad to the eyes". The flowers were thought of as small and ugly.

Zinnias

Blossom watching
Every April in Japan, people sit under cherry trees to watch the falling pink blossoms. This tradition is called "O-hanami" or "flower viewing". It's believed that good energy flows from the tree to the people sitting beneath.

Sticky solutions

In the 16th century, a liquid found in bluebell roots and bulbs was commonly used to glue pages into books.

Flower dye

The chemical that gives marigolds their bright orange petals can be used to dye clothes and hair.

Marigolds *

Floral soap

The soapwort flower takes its name from the fact that its leaves produce a soapy lather when rubbed.

Soapwort was once used as soap.

Seed stuffing

Milkweed seeds are attached to hairs that are so lightweight, they were originally used to stuff lifejackets.

Milkweed seeds

A late developer

The rare *Puya raimondii* plant doesn't flower until it's 150 years old. After that, it dies.

Rare types of tulip bulbs were once sold for their own weight in gold.

Tulipmania

During the 17th century, "tulipmania" swept Holland. Tulips were so valuable that certain types were used as money, with their value changing daily.

Masters of disguise

Stone plants look like small pebbles, which stops hungry animals from eating them.

Stone plants

INDEX

ACKNOWLEDGEMENTS

Managing designer: Karen Tomlins
Artwork co-ordinator: Louise Breen
Website advisor: Lisa Watts
Americanization by Carrie Armstrong

PHOTO CREDITS (t = top, m = middle, b = bottom, l = left, r = right)
1 IPS/Alamy; 3(m) 2004 Digital Vision; 4 & 5(b) 2004 Digital Vision;
7(r) Historical Picture Archive/CORBIS, (b) Photodisc/Getty Images;
8(m) Realimage/Alamy; 29(r) Photodisc/Getty Images; 37(r) Jon Rogers;
41(r) Jon Rogers; 49(t) Photodisc/Getty Images; 53(l) 2004 Digital Vision;
55(b) archivberlin Fotoagentur GmbH/Alamy;
56(l) photolibrary.com/OSF

ADDITIONAL ILLUSTRATORS David Ashby, Graham Austin, Bob Bampton, David Baxter,
Andrew Beckett, Joyce Bee, Isabelle Bowring, Wendy Bramall, Paul Brooks, Mark Burgess, Hilary Burn,
Liz Butler, Frankie Coventry, Patrick Cox, Kevin Dean, Sarah De Ath, Michelle Emblem, Denise Finney,
Sarah Fox-Davies, Nigel Frey, Sheila Galbraith, Will Giles, Victoria Gooman, Victoria Gordon,
David Hurrell, Ian Jackson, Roger Kent, Colin King, Deborah King, Mick Loates, Andy Martin,
Uwe Mayer, Rob McCaig, Dee McLean, Dee Morgan, David Nash, Gillian Platt, Cynthia Pow,
David Quinn, Charles Raymond, Maggie Silver, Gwen Simpson, Ralph Stobart, George Thompson,
Joan Thompson, Joyce Tuhill, Sally Volke, Phil Weare, James Woods